BILBAO

Travel Guide 2024

Lucy T. Dunaway

Guggenheim

Casilda Iturriza

Zeanuri

Puente de la Muza

5

Enekuri Motor
LUTXANA-ENEKURI
Zangroiz
N-637
MONTE SAN PABLO AUZOA
BI-711
14
ELORRIETA
BI-604
SAN IGNAZIO
BI-3741
BI-3741
Artxanda-Ugasko Tunela
Artxanda-Salbe Tunela
BI-3741
BANDERAS MENDIA AUZOA
DEUSTO
IBARREKOLANDA
ARANGOITI
Agirre Lehendakariaren Etorb.
Deustuko Unibertsitatea
119
5
Guggenheim Bilbao Museoa
Botica Vieja
118
Bilboko Arte Ederren Museoa
OLABEAGA
INDAUTXU
Basurtuko Unibertsitate Ospitalea
Azkuna Zentroa (Alhóndiga Bilbao)
ABANDO
A-8
BASURTO-ZORROZA
Silken Indautxu hotela
MASUSTEGI-MONTE CARAMELO
BIVA Bilbao - Plaza de Toros de Vista Alegre
N-634
ERREKALDE
Bilbo Arena Kirol Jauregia
Eskurtze BHI
Mirador Arraiz
Mercadona
SAN ADRIÁN
Betolatza Parkea
A-8
Errekaldeko Kiroldegia Bilbao Kirolak
116
115 A

N-637
14
N-637
BI-3741
BI-3741
Artxanda-Ugasko Tunela
Artxanda-Salbe Tunela
BI-3741
DEUSTO
ARANGOITI
Artxandako
Agirre Lehendakariaren Etorb.
Deustuko Unibertsitatea
LORATEGI-HIRI
Guggenheim Bilbao Museoa
BI-625
Botica Vieja
URIBARRI
Bilboko Arte Ederren Museoa
INDAUTXU
Azkuna Zentroa (Alhóndiga Bilbao)
ABANDO
Etxebarria Parkea
CASCO VIEJO
Silken Indautxu hotela
BIVA Bilbao - Plaza de Toros de Vista Alegre
Erriberako Merkatua
N-634
ATXURI
BEGOÑA
Bilbo Arena Kirol Jauregia
ERREKALDE
Eskurtze BHI
Hotel Gran Bilbao
Mercadona
A-8
SAN ADRIÁN
Errekaldeko Kiroldegia Bilbao Kirolak
116
N-634
115 A
ITURRIGORRI - PEÑASCAL
116C
115 B
Mendipe erretegia
LA PEÑA

Copyright Page

All rights reserved. No part of this publication may be reproduced, stored in a retrieval system, or transmitted in any form or by any means, electronic, mechanical, photocopying, recording, or otherwise, without prior written permission of Lucy T. Dunaway. The information contained in this publication is believed to be accurate and reliable; however, Lucy T. Dunaway does not assume any responsibility for any errors or omissions.

Copyright © 2024 Lucy T. Dunaway

Table of Contents

INTRODUCTION — 13
   History and Culture — 16
   Geography and Climate — 19

CHAPTER 1: Planning Your Trip — 21
   Best Time to Visit — 21
   How to Get There — 23
   Visa Requirements — 25

CHAPTER 2: Getting Around Bilbao — 28
   Public Transportation — 28
   Renting a Car — 30
   Walking and Biking — 32

CHAPTER 3: Where to Stay — 35
   Neighborhood Guide — 35
   Recommended Hotels — 37
   Hostels — 39

CHAPTER 4: Exploring Bilbao — 42
   Top Attractions — 42
   Hidden Gems — 44
   Day Trips from Bilbao — 47

CHAPTER 5: Dining and Nightlife — 49
   Local Cuisine and Must-Try Dishes — 49
   Restaurant Recommendations — 51
   Bars and Nightclubs — 53

CHAPTER 6: Shopping in Bilbao — 55
   Markets and Souvenirs — 55
   Shopping Districts — 57

CHAPTER 7: Culture and Entertainment — 60

Museums and Galleries	60
Theatres and Performance Venues	62
CHAPTER 8: Outdoor Activities	**64**
Parks and Gardens	64
Hiking and Nature Excursions	65
CHAPTER 9: Practical Tips	**68**
Safety Tips	68
Language and Communication	69
Currency and Money Matters	71
Useful Phrases in Basque and Spanish	73
Local Etiquette and Customs	76
CHAPTER 10: Sample Itineraries	**79**
7-day Itinerary	79
Honeymoon Itinerary	82
Family Vacation Itinerary	85
CONCLUSION	**89**

INTRODUCTION

The plane dipped low over the rugged Basque coastline, the turquoise waters of the Bay of Biscay sparkling like scattered jewels. A nervous flutter danced in my stomach – a cocktail of excitement and trepidation for the adventure that awaited in Bilbao. Just hours earlier, Bilbao was a name on a map, a whispered suggestion from a well-traveled friend. Now, the imposing silhouette of the Guggenheim Museum, a titan of modern art clad in shimmering titanium, pierced the horizon, promising a city that dared to be different.

As I stepped off the plane, the crisp Basque air invigorated me. Bilbao wasn't what I expected. Sure, there were remnants of its industrial past – sturdy bridges spanning the Nervión River, warehouses with faded paint peeling from their brick facades. But woven into this industrial combination was a vibrant energy, a youthful pulse that hummed beneath the surface. Street art splashed across concrete walls, each vibrant mural a testament to the city's creative spirit. Modern high-rises gleamed beside charming, half-timbered buildings with flower boxes cascading from their balconies.

My first stop was the iconic Guggenheim. Designed by the visionary architect Frank Gehry, the museum itself was a work of art. Its contorted curves and shimmering scales seemed to defy gravity, a whimsical metallic fish dancing on the riverbank. Inside, the vast, light-filled atrium pulsed with energy. Gazing up at Richard Serra's colossal "The Matter of Time," a labyrinth of twisting steel plates, I felt a childlike sense of wonder. Each gallery unveiled a new artistic treasure – vibrant canvases by Rothko, thought-provoking sculptures by Calder, and installations that pushed the boundaries of my imagination.

Leaving the museum, I wandered into the heart of Bilbao's beating soul – Casco Viejo, the Old Town. Narrow cobbled streets snaked through the labyrinthine neighborhood, each corner revealing a hidden gem. The air hung heavy with the intoxicating aroma of sizzling chorizo and freshly baked bread, wafting from the bustling bars lining the plazas. Pintxos, the Basque answer to tapas, filled brightly lit display cases – miniature culinary masterpieces on cocktail sticks, a symphony of flavors that tantalized my taste buds. I nibbled on melt-in-your-mouth jamón ibérico, savored the smoky richness of grilled peppers, and popped juicy olives into my mouth, each bite a delectable explosion of local goodness.

As the sun dipped below the rooftops, casting long shadows across the plazas, I found myself swept up in the infectious energy of the pintxo crawl. Locals and tourists alike hopped from bar to bar, plates piled high with colorful delicacies, laughter, and conversation spilling out onto the cobblestone streets. It felt like a giant family reunion, everyone united by the shared joy of good food, good company, and a vibrant city.

But Bilbao wasn't just about pintxos and art. The next day, I ventured out to explore the Guggenheim's neighboring Bilbao Maritime Museum. Inside, the rich maritime history of the Basque Country came alive. Climbing aboard a meticulously restored whaling ship, I could almost hear the salty spray on my face and imagine the daring voyages of Basque explorers. Interactive exhibits showcased the city's transformation from a gritty industrial port to a modern metropolis.

A visit to Bilbao wouldn't be complete without a journey up Mount Artxanda. Taking the funicular railway, I ascended to the summit, the city sprawling out below me like a miniature model. The crisp mountain air invigorated my lungs as I took in the breathtaking panorama – the ribbon of the Nervión River winding through the cityscape, the Guggenheim Museum gleaming like a beacon, and the rugged Basque mountains forming a dramatic backdrop.

Bilbao surprised me at every turn. It was a city brimming with contradictions – a gritty past juxtaposed with a modern future, traditional charm infused with an avant-garde spirit. It was a city that celebrated life in all its messy, glorious forms – through the art that challenged perceptions and the food that tantalized taste buds.

As I boarded my flight home, I carried more than souvenirs in my luggage. I carried a piece of Bilbao's vibrant spirit – the lingering taste of a perfect pintxo, the echo of laughter in a bustling plaza, and the awe-inspiring image of the Guggenheim against the Basque sunset. Bilbao wasn't just a city I visited; it was a city I experienced, a city that stole a piece of my heart, and a city I know I'll return to again and again.

History and Culture

Bilbao, the beating heart of Basque Country in northern Spain, boasts a rich blend of history and culture, intricately woven together. Let's delve into this vibrant city's past and present.

From Humble Beginnings to Maritime Hub:

Bilbao's story starts modestly. Settlements huddled along the Nervión River as early as the 2nd century, with the Romans even setting up camp here. The city truly blossomed in the Middle Ages, strategically positioned for trade. Ships laden with wool and iron ore, mined from nearby mountains, set sail from Bilbao's port, propelling it into a prominent commercial center.

A Legacy of Industry and Resilience:

The Industrial Revolution ushered in a new era for Bilbao. Iron and steel production boomed, turning the city into a major European industrial hub. The 19th and early 20th centuries saw a bustling cityscape filled with factories and shipyards. However, by the late 20th century, industry declined, leaving scars on Bilbao's landscape.

Rebirth and Artistic Awakening:

Bilbao didn't wallow in its industrial past. Instead, the city embarked on a remarkable transformation. The Guggenheim Museum Bilbao, a futuristic masterpiece designed by Frank Gehry, became the symbol of this rebirth. Opened in 1997, it drew international attention and sparked cultural renewal.

Basque Roots Run Deep:

Bilbao's cultural identity is fiercely Basque. Euskara, the ancient Basque language, is still spoken here, a testament to a proud heritage. The city vibrates with Basque traditions, from lively folk music and energetic dances to a strong sense of community.

A Blend of Old and New:

Today's Bilbao is a captivating blend of old and new. The narrow, charming streets of the Casco Viejo (Old Town) with its historic Santiago Cathedral stand in stark contrast to the Guggenheim's modern marvel. This juxtaposition perfectly embodies Bilbao's spirit – a city that reveres its past while embracing the future.

A Feast for the Senses:

Bilbao's cultural offerings extend beyond museums and architecture. World-class theater productions grace the stage of the Arriaga Theatre. Gastronomy is another highlight. Pintxos, a delectable variety of tapas, is a must-try, best enjoyed while bar-hopping and soaking up the lively atmosphere.

Bilbao's transformation is a story of resilience, innovation, and a deep connection to its roots. It's a city that will surprise you with its cultural richness, historical depth, and undeniable zest for life.

Geography and Climate

Bilbao's location paints a picture of contrasting beauty. The city itself rests at the mouth of the Nervión River, nestled amidst two small mountain ranges averaging around 1,300 feet in elevation. This creates a dramatic backdrop for the urban sprawl, offering pockets of greenery and opportunities for scenic hikes just outside the city center.

Meanwhile, just 10 miles south lies the Bay of Biscay, a powerful force that shapes Bilbao's climate. The Bay's low-pressure systems and mild air masses create an oceanic climate (Cfb on the Köppen climate classification). This translates to moderate temperatures year-round, with summers that are pleasantly warm by Iberian standards but lack the scorching heat found further south in Spain.

Rainfall plays a leading role in Bilbao's weather story. The Bay's influence brings frequent rain throughout the year, with November being the wettest month. Expect a good amount of cloud cover as well, with rainy days accounting for roughly 45% of the year and cloudy days making up another 40%.

Don't pack away your umbrella! Rain is a regular visitor, so be sure to bring waterproof gear. However, the flip side of this coin is a city bursting with lush greenery. The abundant rain nourishes the surrounding mountains and keeps Bilbao's parks and gardens beautifully vibrant.

Winter chills are kept at bay thanks to the maritime influence. Snowfall is rare in the city itself, although the mountain peaks might get a dusting during the colder months. Sleet, however, is a more frequent visitor, particularly during winter.

Bilbao's geography and climate combine to create a unique and inviting destination. Be prepared for some rain, but also embrace the cool sea breezes, the verdant surroundings, and the mild temperatures that make Bilbao a comfortable place to explore year-round.

CHAPTER 1: Planning Your Trip

Best Time to Visit

Picking the perfect time to visit depends on what you crave from your trip. Here's a breakdown to help you decide:

Sun Seekers and Beach Bums (June-August):

Bilbao basks in its warmest weather during these summer months. The average temperature hovers around a pleasant 25°C (77°F), ideal for exploring the city and soaking up the sun on the beaches of La Concha and Ondarreta. However, keep in mind this is peak tourist season, so expect livelier crowds and potentially higher prices.

Shoulder Season Explorers (May, September):

If you prefer comfortable temperatures with fewer crowds, May and September offer a sweet spot. The weather is mild, perfect for strolling through the Guggenheim or venturing out on day trips. You'll also find better deals on flights and accommodations compared to peak summer. Plus, May coincides with the

Aste Nagusia festival, a lively celebration of Basque culture.

Festival Fanatics (August):

If immersing yourself in local festivities is your priority, aim for mid-August. This is when Bilbao explodes with the Semana Grande, a week-long extravaganza filled with bullfighting (not for the faint of heart!), concerts, parades, and a giant open-air market. Just be prepared to book your accommodation well in advance as this is a popular time for Spanish travelers as well.

Culture Vultures (April, October-November):

Bilbao's cultural scene thrives year-round, but spring and autumn offer a delightful atmosphere for exploration. The spring showers bring a vibrant green to the surrounding hills, and the crowds are thinner. October boasts the BIME (Bilbao International Music Experience) festival, a haven for music lovers. Don't miss the Bilbao Mendi Film Festival in December, showcasing the best adventure and mountain films.

Budget Travelers (November-March):

If you're on a tighter budget, consider visiting Bilbao during the off-season (November to March). Flights and accommodation prices hit their lowest during this time, and the city offers a more relaxed pace. Be prepared for some rain, especially in April, but the mild temperatures make sightseeing comfortable.

Ultimately, the best time to visit Bilbao depends on your preferences. Whether you crave sunshine and festivals or cultural immersion and budget-friendly deals, Bilbao has a season to match your travel style.

How to Get There

Getting to Bilbao is easy, with a variety of options to suit your travel style and budget.

Flying into Bilbao:

Bilbao Airport (BIO), conveniently located just 12 kilometers outside the city center, is the most popular entry point for international travelers. Numerous airlines offer direct flights to Bilbao from major European cities, as well as some destinations within Spain. Once you arrive, the efficient public transportation system connects the airport to the city center in about 15 minutes via bus.

Taxis are readily available at the airport for a quicker, albeit slightly more expensive, journey into town.

Train Travel:

For a scenic journey, consider arriving by train. While there are no direct high-speed train connections to Bilbao from other major Spanish cities, you can take a regional train from nearby Santander or connect through Madrid. The train station is well-located in Bilbao, placing you within walking distance of many central attractions.

Bus Travel:

For budget-minded travelers, long-distance buses offer a comfortable and affordable way to reach Bilbao. Major bus companies operate routes from various Spanish cities and some European destinations. While journey times can be longer than flying or taking the train, the bus network provides a reliable and convenient option.

Road Tripping:

If you crave the freedom of exploration, consider driving to Bilbao. The city is well-connected by Spain's excellent highway network. The A-8 motorway provides a direct route from western France and eastern Spain. For those arriving from other parts of Spain, Bilbao is easily accessible via major highways.

Choosing the Best Option:

The best way to get to Bilbao depends on your priorities. Flying is the fastest choice if time is of the essence. Train travel offers a scenic alternative, while buses provide a budget-friendly choice. Road-tripping allows for flexibility and exploration along the way.

Additional Tips:

- Consider booking your flights, train tickets, or bus reservations in advance, especially during peak season.
- Research Bilbao's public transportation options before you arrive to ensure a smooth transition from the airport, train station, or bus terminal to your accommodation.
- If you're driving, be sure to research parking options in Bilbao, as street parking can be limited in the city center.

Visa Requirements

Bilbao, like all of Spain, sits within the Schengen Area. This means that if you're a citizen of a European Union member country, Iceland, Liechtenstein, Norway, or

Switzerland, you won't need a visa to visit for stays under 90 days.

For travelers from other countries, visa requirements can vary depending on your nationality. Here's a quick breakdown:

No visa required: You can enter Spain visa-free for up to 90 days within 180 days if your country has a visa waiver agreement with the Schengen Area. Check with your nearest Spanish embassy or consulate to see if your country is on the list.

Schengen visa required: If your country isn't on the visa waiver list, you'll need to apply for a Schengen Visa before your trip. This visa allows you to travel freely within the Schengen Area for the duration of its validity. You can typically apply at your home country's Spanish embassy or consulate.

Important things to remember:

- Visa requirements can change, so it's always best to double-check the latest information with the Spanish authorities well before your trip.
- Even if you don't need a visa, you may still need to show proof of onward travel and sufficient funds for your stay.

- Be sure to check the validity of your passport - it should generally be valid for at least three months beyond your intended stay in Spain.
- For a smooth entry process, ensure you have all the necessary documentation in order. A little advanced planning can save you time and hassle upon arrival in vibrant Bilbao.

CHAPTER 2: Getting Around Bilbao

Public Transportation

Bilbao boasts a public transportation system that's the envy of many Spanish cities. It's clean, efficient, and affordable, making it a breeze to navigate the city and its surrounding areas. Here's your lowdown on the main players:

Metro Bilbao: The metro is the city's workhorse, with three lines crisscrossing Bilbao and reaching several neighboring towns. Its modern stations are easily accessible, and the trains are frequent and reliable.

Bilbobus: This extensive network of buses covers just about every corner of Bilbao. With over 40 lines and hundreds of stops, you're never far from a Bilbobus that can whisk you to your destination.

Tram: Bilbao's single tram line cuts through the heart of the city, connecting many of the must-see sights, like the Guggenheim Museum and the Ribera Market. It's a fantastic option for sightseeing and enjoying the city's vibrant atmosphere.

Tickets and Passes: The Barik card is your key to unlocking Bilbao's public transportation system. It's a rechargeable card that works on all metro, tram, and bus lines. You can purchase an anonymous Barik card for a small fee and top it up as needed.

Beyond the City Limits: Bilbao's integrated transportation system extends beyond the city center. Bizkaibus, a separate network of provincial buses, connects Bilbao to the wider Biscay province, allowing you to explore charming towns and coastal villages.

Tips for Using Public Transportation:

- Grab a map: Metro Bilbao and Bilbobus provide handy maps that showcase the different lines and stops.
- Plan your trip: Bilbao's public transportation website has a journey planner tool that helps you map your route and estimate travel times [Bilbao Public Transportation Website].
- Validate your ticket: Remember to validate your Barik card at the designated machines before boarding the metro, tram, or bus.
- Night owls rejoice: Bilbao offers a night bus service on weekends, so you can keep exploring after dark.

Renting a Car

Bilbao is a vibrant city, but to truly explore the heart of Basque Country, consider renting a car. Here's what you need to know:

Car Rental Companies:

Bilbao boasts several major international rental companies like Sixt, Europcar, and Budget, alongside local businesses. Look around for the greatest offer that meets your needs and price range.

Picking Up Your Car:

You can pick up your rental car directly at Bilbao Airport for maximum convenience, or opt for a downtown location that might offer lower rates. Consider how much luggage you have and how comfortable you are navigating city streets to make this decision.

Types of Cars:

Bilbao offers a variety of rental cars. If you're planning on sticking to the city itself, a compact car is a good choice for navigating narrow streets and finding parking. If you plan on venturing into the Basque countryside, consider a sturdier vehicle that can handle mountain roads, especially if traveling during winter.

Things to Consider:

International Driving Permit: While not always mandatory, an International Driving Permit (IDP) is highly recommended, especially if you're pulled over by police.

Insurance: Be sure to understand the insurance coverage included in your rental rate and consider if additional coverage is necessary for peace of mind.

Tolls: Some motorways in Spain have tolls. Ensure you understand the payment system before hitting the road. Many rental companies offer pre-paid toll options.

Navigation: Download offline maps or invest in a GPS device, as data connectivity can be spotty in rural areas.

Driving in Bilbao:

Spanish drivers are known for being assertive. Familiarize yourself with traffic signs and regulations beforehand. Pay attention to one-way streets and pedestrian zones, which are plentiful in the city center.

Parking: On-street parking in Bilbao can be scarce and expensive. Public parking garages are a good alternative, though be aware they can fill up quickly, especially on weekends.

Benefits of a Rental Car:

With a rental car, you have the freedom to explore charming Basque villages, stunning coastal scenery, and the majestic Pyrenees mountains at your own pace. You can also escape the crowds and discover hidden gems off the beaten path.

Walking and Biking

The Nervión River that snakes through its heart pulsates with energy, and the locals themselves embrace an active lifestyle. So, ditch the tour buses and explore Bilbao at your own pace, either on foot or by bike.

Walking:

The Casco Viejo (Old Town): Immerse yourself in Bilbao's rich history by getting lost in the charming labyrinthine streets of the Casco Viejo. Admire the architectural gems like the Santiago Cathedral and wander through the Ribera Market, a feast for the senses with its overflowing stalls of fresh produce and local delicacies.

The Riverside Ramble: The Guggenheim Museum is undoubtedly Bilbao's crown jewel, but don't stop there. Take a stroll along the riverside promenade, enjoying the ever-changing vistas of the Nervión River. Spot the iconic Zubizuri footbridge, resembling a white flower, and admire the architectural prowess of the Euskalduna Conference Centre and Concert Hall.

The Ensanche Expansion: Bilbao's transformation from an industrial town to a modern metropolis is best witnessed in the Ensanche district. Walk along the wide Gran Vía, lined with grand 19th-century buildings, and marvel at the neo-classical Arriaga Theatre. Take a detour to peek into the Arenal area, a vibrant hub brimming with pintxos bars and trendy cafes.

Biking:

Bilbao is a cyclist's paradise with a network of dedicated bike lanes and car-free zones.

Riverside Ride: Embark on a scenic cycling adventure along the Nervión River. The mostly flat مسير (masir, meaning path) allows you to glide effortlessly, taking in the sights from the Guggenheim Museum to the Bizkaia Bridge.

Bilbao's Green Lungs: Escape the city center and explore Bilbao's greener side. Cycle paths weave through Etxebarri Park, offering a tranquil escape, or head further north to Mount Artxanda for a challenging climb rewarded with breathtaking panoramic views.

Bilbao to Getxo: For a more adventurous outing, rent a bike and explore the neighboring coastal town of Getxo. Cycle along the scenic Abra Bay, stopping to admire the charming beaches and the Puente Colgante, a majestic hanging transporter bridge.

CHAPTER 3: Where to Stay

Neighborhood Guide

Here's a guide to some of Bilbao's must-visit districts:

Casco Viejo: A Time Capsule of Charm

Bilbao's beating heart lies in Casco Viejo, the old town. Wander its narrow, medieval streets lined with pintxo bars overflowing with delicious bite-sized Basque treats. Marvel at the imposing Santiago Cathedral, a Gothic masterpiece. Soak up the lively atmosphere in Plaza Nueva, the town's central square, buzzing with locals and tourists alike.

Abando: Modern Marvels on the Riverfront

Across the Nervión River, Abando showcases Bilbao's modern transformation. The iconic Guggenheim Museum, a sculptural marvel in titanium, is the star attraction. Explore its vast collection of contemporary art, then take a stroll along the riverfront, admiring the futuristic architecture like the Zubizuri footbridge.

Indautxu: Bustling Hub with Hidden Delights

Indautxu offers a delightful mix of business and leisure. Discover high-end stores lining the streets, then delve into the serene Doña Casilda Park, a green haven in the heart of the city. Foodies will love browsing the Indautxu Market, brimming with fresh, local produce. In the evening, head to the bars and restaurants lining Calle Alameda for a taste of Bilbao's nightlife.

Deusto: A Buzzing University District

Deusto, home to the University of Deusto, exudes a youthful energy. Explore the riverside promenade, a popular spot for joggers and cyclists. Catch a concert or a play at the iconic Euskalduna Conference Centre and Concert Hall. In the evenings, the neighborhood comes alive with students socializing in the many bars and cafes.

Castaños: An Up-and-Coming Local Haven

For an authentic Bilbao experience, head to Castaños. This working-class neighborhood offers a glimpse into local life. Take a stroll along the Evaristo Churruca promenade, enjoying stunning river views. Sample traditional Basque cuisine in the many family-run restaurants, and soak up the unpretentious charm of this up-and-coming area.

Recommended Hotels

Whether you crave a luxurious spa retreat or a modern haven close to the action, you'll find the perfect place to rest your head in this vibrant Basque city.

Gran Hotel Domine Bilbao: This ultra-modern hotel in the city center is a design aficionado's dream. Sleek rooms boast floor-to-ceiling windows, and the rooftop terrace offers panoramic city views. Guests can unwind at the on-site spa or savor delectable dishes at the hotel's gourmet restaurant.

Address: Mazarredo Zumarkalea, 61

Price: Starts from €167 per night (subject to change)

Hotel Carlton: Steeped in Bilbao's rich history, this elegant hotel occupies a prime location in Plaza Moyua. It exudes classic charm with its grand facade and opulent interiors. Spacious rooms offer a haven of comfort, while the hotel boasts a renowned restaurant and a sophisticated bar.

Address: Plaza Federico Moyúa, 4

Price: Starts from €127 per night (subject to change)

Petit Palace Arana: This charming boutique hotel sits in a quiet corner of the Abando district. Combining modern amenities with a touch of local flair, it offers a personalized stay. The friendly staff is always happy to recommend hidden gems of the city. Don't miss the chance to enjoy a delicious breakfast on the hotel's beautiful patio.

Address: Arenal, 13

Price: Starts from €100 per night (subject to change)

Ibis Bilbao Centro: Ideal for budget-conscious travelers, this Ibis outpost offers clean and comfortable rooms in a central location. It's perfect for those who want to explore the city on foot and appreciate a good value for money. The hotel provides a complimentary breakfast to kickstart your day.

Address: Alameda Mazarredo, 11

Price: Starts from €60 per night (subject to change)

Hotel Artetxe: Located in the heart of Bilbao's Old Town, this historic hotel offers a unique stay steeped in local character. Housed in a beautifully restored

19th-century building, it features charming rooms with exposed beams and modern amenities. The hotel's on-site restaurant serves traditional Basque cuisine in a cozy setting.

Address: Boteros Kalea, 11

Price: Starts from €80 per night (subject to change)

Hostels

Here's a rundown to help you find your ideal Bilbao hostel crashpad:

Quartier Bilbao Hostel: This lively spot boasts free breakfast, a shared kitchen, and a terrace – perfect for fueling up and planning adventures with fellow travelers. Plus, its central location puts you right in the thick of the action.

Botxo Gallery Hostel: Embrace Bilbao's creative spirit at this trendy hostel. Think colorful dorms, a chill lounge, and a communal kitchen to whip up meals and mingle with your new travel crew. Bonus: free Wi-Fi and breakfast to keep you connected and energized.

Bilbao Hostel: If you're all about stretching your travel euros, Bilbao Hostel delivers. This no-frills option offers free breakfast and Wi-Fi, a guest kitchen for budget-conscious cooks, and even on-site gardens for a touch of greenery.

Poshtel Bilbao: This upscale hostel strikes the perfect balance between style and affordability. Think comfy beds in a stylish setting, an on-site bar and restaurant for refueling after a day of exploring, and even a sauna to unwind those sightseeing muscles.

Beyond the Dorms:

Many Bilbao hostels also offer private rooms for those seeking a bit more privacy. This can be a great option for couples or friends traveling together who still want to enjoy the social atmosphere of a hostel.

Insider Tips:

- Book in advance: Bilbao is a popular destination, especially during peak season. To secure your spot in your preferred hostel, book a few weeks or even months in advance.
- Consider location: Think about what you want to be close to – museums, nightlife, or public transport – when choosing your hostel. Most

Bilbao hostels are centrally located, making it easy to explore the city on foot.
- Embrace the social scene: Hostels are a fantastic way to meet fellow travelers and share experiences. Don't be shy – strike up conversations in the common areas, join organized activities, or simply chat with your roommates.

CHAPTER 4: Exploring Bilbao

Top Attractions

Here are some of the must-see attractions that will have you falling in love with this vibrant Basque city:

Guggenheim Museum Bilbao: This architectural masterpiece, designed by Frank Gehry, is a true showstopper. Its swirling titanium exterior houses an impressive collection of modern and contemporary art. Even if museums aren't your thing, the Guggenheim's unique design is worth a visit.

Casco Viejo (Old Town): Immerse yourself in Bilbao's rich history by wandering the narrow streets of Casco Viejo. This charming neighborhood boasts ancient churches like the Santiago Cathedral, bustling squares like Plaza Nueva, and the Ribera Market, a haven for fresh, local produce and delicious pintxos (Basque tapas).

Bilbao Fine Arts Museum: For a deeper dive into art history, head to the Bilbao Fine Arts Museum. Housing an extensive collection spanning centuries, the museum showcases works by Spanish masters like Goya and El Greco, alongside European artistic legends.

Azkuna Zentroa: This multifunctional center, housed in a former wine warehouse, is a haven for creativity. It combines a modern art gallery with a theater, cinema, and concert hall. Even if you don't catch a performance, the building's striking architecture is worth exploring.

Puppy: Standing guard outside the Guggenheim Museum is Jeff Koons' famous floral sculpture, Puppy. This playful and colorful giant dog sculpture made entirely of flowers is a popular spot for photos and a symbol of Bilbao's artistic spirit.

Puente Zubizuri (White Bridge): This elegant white bridge, designed by Santiago Calatrava, is a modern marvel. Take a stroll across it for stunning views of the Nervión River and the city skyline.

Doña Casilda Iturrizar Park: Escape the urban buzz and unwind in the sprawling Doña Casilda Iturrizar Park. Lush greenery, ponds, and charming sculptures create a peaceful oasis perfect for a picnic or a leisurely walk.

Euskalduna Palace: This striking glass and steel structure houses a concert hall, conference center, and theater. The Euskalduna Palace is a major venue for cultural events and performances, and even if you don't have tickets, it's worth admiring its futuristic architecture.

Hidden Gems

beneath the city's modern facade lies a treasure trove of hidden experiences waiting to be discovered. So, ditch the tourist throngs and delve into these secret gems that will make your Bilbao visit truly unforgettable.

A Dive into Basque History: The Basque Museum

Sure, the Guggenheim is an architectural marvel, but for a deeper understanding of Basque culture and heritage, head to the Basque Museum. Tucked away in a 17th-century building, it offers a fascinating glimpse into the region's unique traditions, from prehistoric artifacts to contemporary Basque art.

Time Travel at Atxuri and Abando Train Stations

Bilbao's transformation from an industrial giant to a cultural hub is beautifully captured in its contrasting train stations. The grand neo-classical Atxuri station evokes a bygone era, while the ultra-modern Abando station reflects the city's forward-thinking spirit. Take a moment to appreciate both – a visual history lesson in a nutshell.

A Feast for the Senses: Mercado de la Ribera

Indulge your inner foodie at the immense Mercado de la Ribera, Europe's largest indoor market. Lose yourself in the vibrant chaos as you weave past stalls overflowing with fresh produce, colorful pintxos (Basque tapas), and delectable local delicacies. Don't miss the chance to sample some – it's a culinary adventure for the senses.

A Refreshing Dip with a View: Azkuna Zentroa's Rooftop Pool

For an experience that's both unique and invigorating, take a dip in the rooftop pool at Azkuna Zentroa, a former wine warehouse transformed into a cultural center. Imagine swimming with the Bilbao cityscape as your backdrop, and don't forget to look down – swimmers glide gracefully above the unsuspecting pedestrians below!

A Colorful Escape: The Neighborhood of Irala

Escape the urban grid and discover the charming Irala district. A world away from Bilbao's modern architecture, Irala boasts rows of brightly colored, early 20th-century houses with a distinct English influence. Take a stroll, admire the unique architecture, and feel transported to a different time and place.

A Chill Pill by the River: Zorrotzaurre's Chill-Out Zone

For a dose of laid-back charm, head to the Zorrozaurre peninsula's Chill-Out Zone. This unexpected urban oasis boasts a DIY vibe, with seating crafted from recycled materials and a stunning view of the Nervión River. It's the perfect spot to unwind, soak up the sun, and experience Bilbao at a slower pace.

Explore Bilbao by Canoe

Bilbao isn't just a city to explore on foot. Paddle your way through its canals and discover a fresh perspective. A canoe trip allows you to navigate beneath iconic bridges, glide past historical landmarks, and appreciate the city's architectural wonders from a unique vantage point.

A Culinary Gem: Sua San Restaurant

After a day of exploration, reward yourself with a delectable meal at Sua San. This hidden gem, situated near the Guggenheim, offers a modern take on traditional Basque cuisine. Savor fresh, seasonal ingredients prepared with finesse, and enjoy a warm, inviting atmosphere.

A Step Back in Time: Café Iruña

For a taste of Bilbao's traditional side, step into the elegant Café Iruña. Established in 1903, this iconic establishment boasts a charming Belle Epoque atmosphere. Sip on a coffee, indulge in a slice of their famous cheesecake, and soak up the local energy – it's a Bilbao institution not to be missed.

Day Trips from Bilbao

Lace-up your walking shoes, fire up your taste buds, and let's delve into some unforgettable day trips from Bilbao:

San Sebastian: A Foodie Paradise - A short hop away, San Sebastian is a haven for gourmands. Pintxos (bite-sized Basque tapas) line vibrant bars, and Michelin-starred restaurants tempt with innovative cuisine. Explore the charming Old Town, wander La Concha beach, and soak in the lively atmosphere.

Gaztelugatxe: Dramatic Dragonstone - Channel your inner Daenerys Targaryen with a visit to San Juan de Gaztelugatxe, a hermitage perched atop a dramatic islet. Climb the 241 steps to the chapel, rewarded by breathtaking coastal views. Be sure to snap a photo with the imposing rock formations as your backdrop.

Gernika: Peace and History - Steeped in symbolism, Gernika is a town etched in history. Explore the imposing Assembly House, a UNESCO World Heritage Site, and witness the poignant "Guernica" bombing mural replica by Picasso. Delve into the Basque culture and the region's fight for peace.

The Coast of Biscay: Seaside Charm - Escape the city bustle and explore the charming coastal towns dotting the Bay of Biscay. Bermeo, a historic fishing village, boasts a lively harbor and a fascinating maritime museum. Mundaka, a surfer's haven, offers stunning beaches and a chance to witness world-class waves.

La Rioja: Wine & Gastronomy - Venture inland to La Rioja, Spain's premier wine region. Sample world-renowned tempranillo grapes at renowned wineries, many offering tours and tastings. Pair your exploration with delicious regional cuisine, creating a day trip that tantalizes the palate.

Biarritz & Saint-Jean-de-Luz: French Flair - Feeling a touch of wanderlust? Cross the border into France and discover the delightful seaside towns of Biarritz and Saint-Jean-de-Luz. Biarritz boasts a sophisticated charm, while Saint-Jean-de-Luz offers a charming harbor and delicious French pastries.

CHAPTER 5: Dining and Nightlife

Local Cuisine and Must-Try Dishes

Get ready to tantalize your taste buds with fresh seafood, hearty stews, and the ever-present pintxos.

Pintxos: A Pintxos Paradise

Forget tapas! In Bilbao, it's all about pintxos, the Basque answer to small plates. These delectable bites usually speared on a toothpick, come in endless varieties. Picture fluffy bread topped with slivers of cured ham, creamy cheese, or piquant peppers. Indulge in miniature works of art, from sizzling shrimp skewers to decadent potato croquettes. Pintxos hopping, or going from bar to bar sampling these delights, is a beloved local tradition.

Bacalao al Pil-Pil: A Basque Treasure

Basque cuisine is all about fresh, seasonal ingredients, and bacalao al pil-pil perfectly exemplifies this philosophy. This iconic dish features codfish simmered in olive oil with garlic and fiery chiles. The result? Delectable, flaky fish bathed in a rich, creamy sauce – a must-try for any seafood lover.

Marmitako: A Hearty Stew for the Soul

For a taste of Basque comfort food, delve into a steaming bowl of marmitako. This soul-warming stew traditionally features tuna, potatoes, peppers, and onions simmered to perfection. The flavors meld beautifully, creating a hearty and satisfying dish that's perfect for cooler evenings.

Txuleton: A Carnivore's Dream

Meat lovers, rejoice! Txuleton, a colossal bone-in ribeye steak, is a carnivore's dream come true. This succulent steak is typically grilled over open flames, resulting in a perfectly seared exterior and a juicy, flavorful interior. Be warned, portions are generous, so come hungry or consider sharing.

Sweet Endings: Basque Desserts

Bilbao doesn't disappoint when it comes to sweet treats. Don't miss the oportunidad (opportunity) to try pastel vasco, a traditional Basque cake. This dense yet melt-in-your-mouth dessert features a buttery crust filled with rich almond cream. For a lighter option, Carolina, a puff pastry filled with custard, is a delightful choice.

Restaurant Recommendations

Here's a guide to tantalize your taste buds and help you navigate Bilbao's delicious landscape:

Indulge in Classic Basque Cuisine:

Restaurante Nido Bilbao: This modern restaurant with exposed brick walls offers a taste of traditional Basque cuisine. Sink your teeth into a juicy txuleton (a hefty Basque steak) or savor their fresh seafood dishes.

Gure Toki: Embrace the contemporary side of Basque cooking at Gure Toki. Their menu features innovative takes on classic pintxos (bite-sized Basque tapas) alongside delicious regional wines.

Restaurante Pentxo: For a quintessential Bilbao experience, head to Restaurante Pentxo. This traditional spot is a haven for pintxos lovers, offering a wide variety of these flavorful skewers alongside classic local fare.

Explore International Flavors:

Kali Orexi by Labocatorio: Craving a taste of the Mediterranean? Kali Orexi offers a delightful journey through Greek cuisine. From succulent gyros to flavorful moussaka, this restaurant is a delicious escape.

Il Basilico: Bilbao boasts a hidden gem for Italian food lovers. Il Basilico serves up fresh, authentic Italian dishes in a cozy and welcoming atmosphere.

Fine Dining Delights:

Bilbao caters to discerning palates with Michelin-starred establishments. Consider booking in advance for an unforgettable culinary experience at:

Azurmendi: This renowned restaurant offers a progressive take on Basque cuisine, showcasing locally sourced ingredients with innovative techniques.

Ola Martín Berasategui: Experience the culinary artistry of Martín Berasategui at his namesake restaurant. Expect an explosion of flavors and textures in a luxurious setting.

Bars and Nightclubs

Here's a glimpse into the diverse world of Bilbao's after-dark offerings:

Casco Viejo: Dive into the heart of Bilbao's historic center, where narrow streets are lined with atmospheric bars buzzing with locals.

Bodega Iratxe: This traditional bar offers a quintessential Bilbao experience. Sample local pintxos (Basque tapas) alongside a glass of Rioja wine.

El Perro Chico: A lively spot known for its friendly atmosphere and eclectic music selection, perfect for a casual night out.

Pozas and Indautxu: These trendy neighborhoods boast a sophisticated bar scene with a focus on innovative cocktails and international vibes.

Sir Winston Churchill Pub: As the name suggests, this British-style pub offers a wide range of whiskeys and beers in a classy setting.

Gin Fizz Bilbao Cocktail Bar: For the cocktail aficionado, Gin Fizz boasts an impressive selection of creative concoctions served by expert bartenders.

Nightclubs: Bilbao's club scene comes alive later at night, with venues catering to different musical preferences.

Cotton Club: A longstanding favorite, Cotton Club offers a pulsating dance floor with a mix of house and electronic music.

Budha Bilbao: This popular disco attracts a young crowd with high-energy dance music and themed nights.

CHAPTER 6: Shopping in Bilbao

Markets and Souvenirs

Here's your guide to navigating Bilbao's markets and finding the perfect souvenirs to commemorate your trip.

Market Marvels:

Mercado de La Ribera: This iconic market, housed in a stunning 19th-century building, is a must-visit for any foodie. Rows upon rows of stalls overflow with the freshest fish, glistening vegetables, and an enticing array of Basque specialties. Be sure to sample the delectable pintxos (skewered tapas) – a delightful way to experience the local cuisine.

Flea Markets: Bilbao bursts with lively flea markets on specific days. Head to the Plaza Nueva on Sundays for a treasure hunt through a sea of second-hand goods and vintage finds. The Dos de Mayo flea market, held on the first Saturday of every month in the Bilbao La Vieja neighborhood, is another gem for uncovering unique trinkets and local crafts.

Open Your Ganbara Market: Located in the heart of Bilbao, this alternative market takes place on Sundays at the old Artiach biscuit factory. Here, you'll find a treasure trove of local produce, handcrafted items by

Basque artisans, and delicious street food – a fantastic way to immerse yourself in Bilbao's creative spirit.

Souvenirs with Soul:

Bilbao's souvenirs go beyond the usual tourist trinkets. Here are some unique finds to bring a piece of the Basque Country home:

Basque Beret (txapela): This iconic headwear, a symbol of Basque culture, comes in various colors and styles. It's a stylish and practical souvenir that will remind you of your Basque adventures.

Ikurrina Flag: This vibrant flag, featuring the green, white, and red stripes of the Basque Country, is a popular souvenir. It's a great way to show your appreciation for the region's rich heritage.

Gourmet Delights: Indulge in a taste of Basque gastronomy with gourmet food items like Idiazabal cheese, Ibarra smoked paprika or a bottle of Rioja wine. These delectable treats are perfect for bringing back a taste of Bilbao for you and your loved ones.

Handcrafted Basque Products: From intricate ceramics and woven baskets to hand-carved wooden items, Bilbao boasts a thriving artisan community. Look out for unique pieces that showcase the region's artistic talent.

Insider Tips:

- Haggling: Don't be afraid to haggle a bit at flea markets for the best prices. It's part of the fun and adds to the market experience.
- Market Hours: Most markets operate during the mornings. Plan your visit accordingly to ensure you don't miss the vibrant atmosphere and fresh offerings.
- Carry Cash: While many vendors accept cards, some may prefer cash, especially at smaller stalls. Always keep a few euros on hand for emergencies.

Shopping Districts

Whether you crave designer labels or unique local finds, the city has a district waiting to be explored. Here's a guide to Bilbao's top shopping areas:

Ensanche: A Touch of Class

Ensanche, Bilbao's elegant central district, is a haven for luxury shoppers. Grand Vía, Marqués del Puerto, and Rodríguez Arias streets, known as the "Golden Mile," boast flagship stores of international brands like Chanel, Armani, and Louis Vuitton. Here, you'll also find El Corte Inglés, Spain's renowned department store, offering a vast selection of fashion, homewares, and electronics.

Casco Viejo: Unveiling Bilbao's Soul

Step into Bilbao's historic heart, Casco Viejo, and discover a charming labyrinth of narrow streets brimming with character. Here, traditional shops selling Basque handicrafts, quirky boutiques showcasing local designers, and family-run businesses offering regional delicacies line the streets. Don't miss the chance to snag a unique piece of Basque jewelry or a hand-painted ceramic as a memento of your trip.

Abandoibarra: Modernity Meets Shopping

Bilbao's modern waterfront district, Abandoibarra, offers a contemporary shopping experience. The architecturally striking Zubiarte shopping center houses a diverse range of stores, from fashion brands like Zara and Mango to electronics stores and specialty shops. For a touch of the local scene, explore the Mercado de la Ribera, a bustling indoor market showcasing fresh produce, gourmet food items, and even flowers.

Beyond the Districts: Unveiling Hidden Gems

Bilbao's shopping scene extends beyond the main districts. Indautxu is a haven for independent stores offering a curated selection of clothing and homeware. For a taste of the alternative scene, explore Castaños, known for its trendy clothing stores and vintage finds.

Bilbao caters to every shopper's fancy, from the high-end fashionista to the treasure hunter seeking unique local finds. So put on your walking shoes, grab your shopping bags, and get ready to discover the vibrant shopping scene that Bilbao has to offer.

CHAPTER 7: Culture and Entertainment

Museums and Galleries

Bilbao's diverse collections offer something for every taste.

Guggenheim Museum Bilbao: This architectural marvel, designed by Frank Gehry, is a landmark in itself. Inside, explore a vast collection of modern and contemporary art, including works by Richard Serra, Jeff Koons, and Eduardo Chillida.

Bilbao Fine Arts Museum: Delve into Spanish and European art from the 12th to the 20th centuries. Admire masterpieces by El Greco, Goya, and Ribera, alongside an impressive Basque art collection. Don't miss the special exhibitions that delve deeper into specific artistic movements or regions.

Euskal Museoa Bilbao (Basque Museum): Immerse yourself in Basque history and culture. This museum showcases traditional costumes, tools, and archaeological finds, providing a fascinating glimpse into the Basque Country's unique identity.

Museo de Arte Sacro (Museum of Sacred Art): Step back in time and explore religious art from the Middle

Ages to the 19th century. Admire religious sculptures, paintings, and goldwork, many from Basque churches and monasteries.

Beyond the Big Names: Bilbao offers a wealth of smaller museums waiting to be discovered. The Itsasmuseum Bilbao showcases maritime history, while the Bizkaia Museum of Archaeology delves into the region's prehistoric past. The Museum of Sacred Art offers a glimpse into religious life, while the Museo Pasos de Semana Santa (Holy Week Museum) displays the elaborate floats used in Bilbao's renowned processions.

For the Art Enthusiast: Several contemporary art galleries dot Bilbao's landscape. Explore the latest works by local and international artists at galleries like Altxerri and CarrerasMugica.

Bilbao Museum Pass: Consider purchasing a Bilbao Museum Pass for discounted entry to many museums and special exhibitions, making your artistic exploration even more rewarding.

Theatres and Performance Venues

From historic stages to modern marvels, there's a venue and a show to enthrall every visitor.

Teatro Arriaga: The crown jewel of Bilbao's theater scene, the Arriaga is a stunning neo-classical building dating back to the 1890s. Its opulent interior sets the stage for world-class opera, ballet, and theatrical productions.

Palacio Euskalduna: This modern marvel is a multi-purpose complex housing a concert hall, theater, and congress center. Catch everything from renowned orchestras to contemporary dance performances here.

Teatro Campos Elíseos: Step back in time at this charming 19th-century theater. Its smaller scale fosters a more intimate atmosphere, perfect for enjoying chamber music recitals or local plays.

Kafe Antzokia: This multi-faceted venue offers a unique blend of experiences. Catch a live band one night, enjoy a Basque culinary adventure the next, and see an up-and-coming performance troupe another.

Beyond the Stage:

Bilbao's performance scene extends beyond traditional theaters. Throughout the year, the city comes alive with street performers, music festivals, and even open-air cinema screenings. Be sure to check local listings to discover what hidden gems await during your visit.

Insider Tip: Many venues offer guided tours, allowing you to peek behind the curtain and discover the fascinating history hidden within these architectural gems.

CHAPTER 8: Outdoor Activities

Parks and Gardens

Whether you crave a quiet picnic spot, a place for the kids to run wild, or a scenic stroll, Bilbao's green spaces have something for everyone.

Doña Casilda Iturrizar Park: This crown jewel of Bilbao's parks is a local favorite. Lush green lawns unfurl beneath a canopy of mature trees, perfect for a leisurely picnic or a game of frisbee. A charming pond, home to a colony of friendly ducks, adds a touch of tranquility. Kids will love the playground, while adults can admire the elegant statues and fountains scattered throughout the park.

Abandoibarra Park: Situated right next to the iconic Guggenheim Museum, Abandoibarra Park offers a unique blend of art and nature. Its modern design incorporates sleek walkways, landscaped gardens, and even a children's play area. Take a break from museum hopping to relax on a park bench and enjoy the views of the Nervión River, or stroll along the riverside promenade for a breath of fresh air.

Miribilla Park: This expansive park on the outskirts of Bilbao is a haven for outdoor enthusiasts. Miles of walking and biking paths wind through rolling hills, offering stunning city views. Sports facilities like tennis courts and a skate park cater to the active traveler, while playgrounds and picnic areas make it a great choice for families.

Albia Lorategiak: Located in the heart of the city, Albia Lorategiak offers a delightful escape from the urban buzz. This charming garden boasts meticulously tended flower beds, shaded walkways, and a central fountain. It's the perfect spot for a quiet afternoon reading a book or simply soaking up the sunshine.

Etxebarria Park: A hidden gem tucked away in the Bilbao La Vieja neighborhood, Etxebarria Park is a tranquil oasis. Mature trees cast dappled shade over winding paths, while a small pond attracts local birdlife. Explore the park's historic past with a visit to the 12th-century hermitage of San Roque, or simply relax on a bench and listen to the gentle murmur of the water.

Hiking and Nature Excursions

Lace-up your boots and get ready to explore dramatic coastlines, serene mountains, and charming villages – all within reach of the city center.

Gaztelugatxe: This iconic islet, topped by a charming hermitage, is a must-do for any nature enthusiast visiting Bilbao. Hike up the winding path with its 241 steps, enjoying the panoramic views of the Bay of Biscay. Don't forget to ring the hermitage bell for good luck!

Urdaibai Biosphere Reserve: Escape the city and delve into this UNESCO-designated reserve. Explore tidal flats teeming with birdlife, hike through lush green meadows, or visit the charming fishing village of Mundaka, famous for its perfect left-hand wave.

Mount Artxanda: Take the funicular railway up Mount Artxanda for breathtaking city views. Hike or bike the trails that crisscross the mountain, offering panoramic vistas of Bilbao and the surrounding countryside. Pack a picnic and enjoy a leisurely lunch amidst the tranquility of nature.

Camino de Santiago: For the dedicated hiker, a section of the world-famous Camino de Santiago pilgrimage route passes through Bilbao. Hike a portion of this historic trail, experiencing rolling Basque countryside, charming villages, and a true sense of cultural immersion.

Beyond the City Limits: Day trips from Bilbao unlock a treasure trove of natural wonders. Explore the majestic Gorbea Massif, hike through the rolling hills of the Ayala

Valley, or visit the nearby seaside town of Getxo with its scenic cliffs and beaches.

Nature for All: Whether you're a seasoned hiker or a casual nature lover, Bilbao offers something for everyone. Guided tours cater to all levels of experience, allowing you to explore the region with a knowledgeable local guide. Rent a bike and explore the scenic Bilbao Estuary, or simply relax in the sprawling Doña Casilda Iturrizar Park, a haven of green space in the heart of the city.

CHAPTER 9: Practical Tips

Safety Tips

Here are some safety tips to keep your trip worry-free:

Be Street Smart: Keep an eye on your belongings, especially in crowded areas like La Ribera Market or on the metro. Avoid carrying excessive amounts of cash or valuables.

Night Owl? Stick to Lit Areas: While Bilbao is generally safe at night, it's always best to stay on well-lit streets, particularly if you're alone. If you're exploring after dark, consider sticking to main avenues or hopping in a taxi.

Areas to Avoid: Bilbao La Vieja, particularly the San Francisco neighborhood, is best explored during the day. While not inherently dangerous, it's an area with a higher concentration of marginal groups and might feel less comfortable at night.

Taxis by Day, Metro by Night: Taxis are a convenient option, especially at night or if you're unfamiliar with the area. During the day, the metro is a clean, efficient, and affordable way to get around. Just be mindful of your belongings in crowded carriages.

Local Knowledge is Power: Don't hesitate to ask friendly locals for directions. Many Bilbainos speak English, especially in tourist areas, and are happy to help.

Trustworthy Rides: Pre-arrange reliable transportation, especially for late-night arrivals. Many hotels offer airport pickups or can recommend reputable taxi companies.

Digital Security: Bilbao offers free Wi-Fi in many public spaces, but be cautious when using open networks. Don't use public Wi-Fi to access private information, such as bank accounts.

Emergency Numbers: Store emergency contact information in your phone, including the local police number (092) and ambulance (112).

Language and Communication

While Spanish is the common thread that binds most of Spain, here, Euskara (Basque) shares the spotlight. This ancient, pre-Indo-European tongue adds a unique layer to the city's identity.

Understanding the Lingo:

Spanish Reigns Supreme: Don't worry, Spanish is widely spoken and understood throughout Bilbao. You'll have no trouble navigating the city with a basic understanding of Spanish phrases. Many locals will even appreciate your attempt, even if it's a bit rusty.

Euskera's Enduring Presence: Euskara signs pepper the streets, menus, and even traffic announcements. While you might not become fluent on your trip, learning a few basic Euskara greetings ("Kaixo" - Hello, "Eskerrik asko" - Thank you) goes a long way. Locals appreciate the effort to acknowledge their heritage.

English? Sometimes: English isn't as prevalent as Spanish, but you'll find it spoken in tourist areas, hotels, and some restaurants. However, relying solely on English might limit your interactions with the warmth of Bilbao's people.

Communication Tips:

Embrace the Challenge: Bilbao's bilingual environment can be a fun puzzle to navigate. There's a certain charm in pointing and smiling, using travel apps to translate, or even learning a few basic Euskara phrases.

Non-verbal Communication: Bilbaoans are friendly and expressive. A smile, a nod, and hand gestures can often bridge the language gap. Don't be afraid to act things out if you get stuck.

Bilbao for the Bilingual: If you're a Spanish speaker, you're in for a treat! Bilbao offers a vibrant Spanish experience, allowing you to fully immerse yourself in the language.

Currency and Money Matters

Bilbao, like the rest of Spain, uses the Euro (€) as its official currency. You'll find bills in denominations of 5, 10, 20, 50, 100, 200, and 500 euros, alongside coins in 1, 2, 5, 10, 20, and 50 cent pieces, and 1 and 2 euro coins.

Deciding on Euros:

Credit Cards: Credit cards are widely accepted in Bilbao, especially in larger stores, restaurants, and hotels. Using your card can offer good exchange rates and convenience, but be sure to check with your bank about any international transaction fees.

ATM Withdrawals: ATMs are plentiful throughout Bilbao, particularly in tourist areas. Withdrawing cash from your bank card at an ATM is a reliable way to get euros, but be aware of potential withdrawal fees from both your home bank and the ATM provider.

Exchanging Currency: While not always the most economical option, currency exchange offices can be handy for getting a small amount of euros upon arrival, especially if you need cash for transportation or a taxi. However, exchange rates at bureaus de change can be less favorable than banks or ATMs.

Tipping:

Tipping in Spain is customary, but not mandatory. In Bilbao, a small gratuity (around 5-10% of the bill) is appreciated in restaurants, especially if you receive good service. For taxis, rounding up the fare is a common practice.

A Few Extra Euros:

Always have a small amount of cash on hand for smaller purchases, public restroom fees, or situations where cards aren't accepted. However, Bilbao is a very card-friendly city, so you likely won't need a large amount of cash throughout your trip.

Useful Phrases in Basque and Spanish

While English is spoken in tourist areas, knowing a few basic phrases in Basque and Spanish will enhance your experience and show respect for the local way of life. Here's a cheat sheet to get you started:

Greetings and Pleasantries:

Basque:

- Kaixo (Kai-sho): Hello (informal)
- Egun on (Eh-gun on): Good morning
- Arratsalde on (Ah-rahts-al-deh on): Good afternoon
- Gabon (Gah-bone): Good evening
- Agur (Ah-goor): Goodbye
- Eskerrik asko (Ehs-keh-rrik ahs-ko): Thank you very much

Spanish:

- Hola (Oh-lah): Hello
- Buenos días (Bwee-nos dee-ahs): Good morning
- Buenas tardes (Bwee-nahs tar-des): Good afternoon
- Buenas noches (Bwee-nahs noh-ches): Good evening

- Adiós (Ah-dee-ohs): Goodbye
- Muchas gracias (Moo-chahs grah-see-ahs): Thank you very much

Getting Around:

Basque:

- Barkatu (Bar-kah-too): Excuse me
- Non dago...? (Non dah-go...?): Where is...? (followed by the place you're looking for)
- Zenbat balio du? (Zen-bat bah-lee-oh doo?): How much is this?

Spanish:

- Lo siento (Loh syeh-ntoh): Excuse me
- ¿Dónde está...? (Don-deh es-tah...?): Where is...? (followed by the place you're looking for)
- ¿Cuánto cuesta? (Cwan-toh cwes-tah?): How much is this?

Dining Delights:

Basque:

- On egin (On eh-gin): Enjoy your meal
- Osasuna! (Oh-sah-soo-nah!): Cheers! (typically used with cider)

Spanish:

- Buen provecho (Bwen pro-veh-cho): Enjoy your meal
- ¡Salud! (Sah-lood!): Cheers!

Bonus Phrases:

Basque:

- Bai (By): Yes
- Ez (Ehs): No

Spanish:

- Sí (See): Yes
- No (No): No

A Few Tips:

- A smile and a friendly attitude go a long way, even if your Basque or Spanish isn't perfect.
- Don't be afraid to try – locals will appreciate your effort to speak their language.
- Pointing and gesturing can help you get by if you're stuck.

Local Etiquette and Customs

To fully immerse yourself in the local experience, brushing up on a few etiquette tips will go a long way.

Greetings and Interactions:

Bilbaoans are known for their warmth and hospitality. A handshake is a standard greeting, but you might also encounter "la besa," two kisses on alternating cheeks. This is common in social situations, especially when introduced to someone new. Addressing people with "señor" (sir) or "señora" (madam) shows respect, especially towards elders or those in service positions.

Dress Code:

Bilbao is a fashion-conscious city. While there's no strict dress code, locals tend to dress smartly casual. Opt for clean, put-together outfits, especially when visiting museums or nicer restaurants. Leave the beachwear for the seaside resorts. Comfort is key, so comfortable shoes are essential for navigating Bilbao's charming, but sometimes hilly, streets.

Dining Do's and Don'ts:

Bilbao's culinary scene is a highlight. Lunch is the main meal of the day, often enjoyed between 2 pm and 4 pm. Dinners tend to be later, starting around 9 pm. Take your time and savor your meals – rushing is considered rude. When splitting the bill, it's customary to offer, but not insist, on paying your share.

Social Etiquette:

Bilbaoans are passionate about conversation, especially when it comes to food, football (soccer), and their beloved Basque culture. A few basic Spanish phrases will be appreciated, and locals are happy to help with pronunciation. If you're unsure about something, err on the side of caution and ask politely.

Respecting the Culture:

Bilbao has a rich cultural heritage. When visiting churches or museums, dress modestly and be mindful of noise levels. Be respectful of local traditions, like the importance of "txikiteo" (bar hopping with pintxos, Basque tapas).

CHAPTER 10: Sample Itineraries

7-day Itinerary

This itinerary blends iconic landmarks with hidden gems, offering a taste of Basque culture, breathtaking landscapes, and, of course, phenomenal food. Lace up your walking shoes and get ready to discover Bilbao!

Day 1: Unveiling the Modern Marvel

Start your adventure at the Guggenheim Museum, a titanium masterpiece that revolutionized Bilbao's skyline. Immerse yourself in the contemporary art collection, then marvel at the intricate architecture. Afterward, stroll along the Nervión River, admiring the whimsical Zubizuri Bridge, nicknamed "Puppy's Playground" for Jeff Koons' iconic floral sculpture. Refuel with a delicious "pintxos" (Basque tapas) crawl in the Casco Viejo (Old Town). Explore narrow cobbled streets lined with charming bars, savoring bite-sized culinary delights alongside friendly locals.

Day 2: Delving into Basque History

Delve into Bilbao's rich past at the Bilbao Fine Arts Museum. Explore an extensive collection spanning centuries, showcasing works by Spanish masters like El Greco and Goya. Next, head to the Santiago Cathedral, a

Gothic gem boasting gargoyle guardians and stained-glass windows. Climb the tower for panoramic city views. In the afternoon, wander through the Arenal district, a bustling commercial center. Immerse yourself in the lively atmosphere and admire the elegant 19th-century architecture. Conclude your day with a traditional Basque dinner, indulging in hearty stews and fresh seafood.

Day 3: A Day Trip to Gaztelugatxe

Gear up for a scenic adventure. Take a day trip to Gaztelugatxe, a dramatic islet crowned by a 10th-century hermitage. Hike up 241 steps, ringing the hermitage bell for good luck. Afterward, explore the charming fishing village of Bermeo, known for its colorful harbor and delicious seafood. Discover the rich maritime heritage of the town by visiting the Fishermen's Museum. Enjoy a fresh seafood lunch with breathtaking harbor views. In the evening, return to Bilbao, unwinding with a relaxing pintxos crawl in a different part of Casco Viejo.

Day 4: Exploring Bilbao's Green Side

Escape the urban buzz and embrace nature. Take the Artxanda Funicular for a scenic climb to Mount Artxanda. Hike through lush greenery, enjoying breathtaking panoramic views of Bilbao. Pack a picnic and find a secluded spot to relax and soak in the fresh air. In the afternoon, visit the Bilbao Maritime Museum, housed in an old shipyard. Learn about Bilbao's industrial past and its fascinating maritime heritage. Afterward, explore the Euskalduna Conference Centre and Concert Hall, a striking architectural marvel overlooking the river.

Day 5: Unveiling Bilbao's Quirky Side

Embrace Bilbao's unconventional spirit. Head to Azkuna Zentroa, a former wine warehouse transformed into a vibrant cultural and leisure center. Explore its unique architecture, housing a contemporary art gallery, a cinema, and a theater. In the afternoon, visit the Bilbao Riverside Museum, showcasing the city's industrial past through historical exhibits and restored machinery. End your day with a performance at the Arriaga Theatre, Bilbao's Grand Opera House, or catch a local show at one of the city's many theaters.

Day 6: A Culinary Journey through Basque Country

Embark on a gastronomic adventure. Take a day trip to a nearby town like Getaria, famous for its txakoli (sparkling white wine) and fresh grilled fish. Sample local specialties and learn about Basque culinary traditions in a cooking class. In the afternoon, explore the town's narrow streets and charming harbor. Return to

Bilbao for a farewell dinner at a Michelin-starred restaurant, savoring the pinnacle of Basque cuisine.

Day 7: Farewell, Bilbao!

Spend your last morning browsing the bustling Ribera Market, a haven for fresh produce, local delicacies, and handcrafted souvenirs. Stock up on tasty treats and unique keepsakes as mementos of your Basque adventure. In the afternoon, head to the airport, taking one last look at Bilbao's captivating skyline.

Honeymoon Itinerary

Bilbao, a city reborn, offers a captivating blend of art, architecture, and Basque charm, perfect for an unforgettable honeymoon escape.

Day 1: Artistic Exploration and Pintxos Paradise

Morning: Start at the iconic Guggenheim Museum. Wander through its modern and contemporary art collections, marveling at the architectural masterpiece designed by Frank Gehry.

Afternoon: Stroll hand-in-hand through Casco Viejo, Bilbao's charming Old Town. Admire the medieval architecture, soak in the lively atmosphere, and discover hidden gems.

Evening: Embark on a 'pintxos' adventure. These bite-sized Basque delicacies are perfect for sharing. Bar hop along the lively streets of Indautxu or Pozas, savoring the diverse flavors and enjoying the local company.

Day 2: Museum Hopping and Coastal Views

Morning: Immerse yourselves in the Bilbao Fine Arts Museum. Explore its vast collection spanning centuries, from Renaissance masterpieces to Basque art.

Afternoon: Take a scenic boat trip along the Nervion River. Enjoy breathtaking views of the city's bridges and the surrounding mountains, capturing romantic moments with a backdrop of the cityscape.

Evening: Savor a delectable dinner at a Michelin-starred restaurant in Bilbao. Indulge in the innovative Basque cuisine, known for its fresh, seasonal ingredients and creative presentations.

Day 3: Seaside Escape and Local Charm

Morning: Take a day trip to the picturesque coastal town of Getxo. Relax on its golden sand beaches, stroll along the scenic promenade, and soak in the fresh sea air.

Afternoon: Visit Puente Bizkaia, a UNESCO World Heritage Site. This transporter bridge, a feat of 19th-century engineering, offers stunning views of the port and surrounding area.

Evening: Enjoy a romantic sunset dinner overlooking the Guggenheim Museum. As the city lights twinkle, reminisce about the day's adventures and create memories that will last a lifetime.

Day 4: Relaxation and Basque Country Flavors

Morning: Pamper yourselves at a traditional Basque spa. Unwind in thermal baths, indulge in relaxing treatments, and rejuvenate together.

Afternoon: Explore the Mercado de la Ribera, Bilbao's bustling market. Immerse yourselves in the sights, sounds, and aromas of fresh produce, local delicacies, and Basque specialties.

Evening: Enjoy a final farewell dinner in the heart of Bilbao. Savor the warmth of Basque hospitality and toast to a honeymoon filled with art, culture, and unforgettable experiences.

Family Vacation Itinerary

From artistic adventures to outdoor explorations, this itinerary packs in five days of unforgettable memories.

Day 1: A Splash of Art and a Taste of History

Morning: Start your adventure at the iconic Guggenheim Museum. Its futuristic architecture is a sight in itself, and the modern and contemporary art collections will spark curiosity in all ages. Look for interactive exhibits and family-friendly tours.

Afternoon: Take a stroll through the Casco Viejo (Old Town). Get lost in the maze of narrow streets lined with pintxos bars, perfect for grabbing a bite of these delicious Basque tapas. Don't miss the imposing Santiago Cathedral, a masterpiece of Gothic architecture.

Evening: Enjoy a traditional Basque dinner. Let your taste buds travel with flavorful dishes like "marmitako" (vegetable and tuna stew) or "bacalao pil pil" (codfish with garlic and chili oil). Most restaurants offer kid-friendly options.

Day 2: Nautical Delights and Mountain Views

Morning: Explore the Bilbao Maritime Museum. Learn about the city's rich maritime history through interactive exhibits, model ships, and fascinating stories. Kids will love exploring the life-sized replica of a traditional Basque whaling boat.

Afternoon: Take a funicular railway ride up Mount Artxanda. Savor the magnificent sweeping views of the city and the mountains in the vicinity. Relax in the park at the summit, have a picnic lunch, and let the kids burn off some energy on the playground.

Evening: Catch a traditional Basque folk performance—a lively experience with energetic music and colorful costumes. Performances often include dancing, singing, and even instrumental displays.

Day 3: A Day Trip to Get Wild

Full Day: Embark on a day trip to Gaztelugatxe, a dramatic islet off the coast of Bilbao. Hike up a steep path with stunning ocean views to reach a charming hermitage perched on the top. Afterward, head to Getaria, a charming coastal town, for a delicious lunch of fresh seafood.

Day 4: Family Fun and Local Flavors

Morning: Take a break from museums and visit the Bilbao Fair. This lively market offers a vibrant array of fresh produce, local crafts, and delicious treats. Kids will love spotting all the colorful foods and unique items. Grab some snacks for a picnic lunch later!

Afternoon: Head to Parque Europa, a sprawling green space with themed gardens representing different European countries. Let the kids run wild on the playgrounds, explore the maze, and enjoy a relaxing picnic lunch amidst the beautiful scenery.

Evening: Catch a family-friendly movie at one of Bilbao's modern cinemas. Most offer shows in English or with subtitles. Enjoy some popcorn and a shared movie experience.

Day 5: Farewell, Bilbao!

Morning: Spend the last morning browsing the shops in the Indautxu district. Find unique souvenirs, local fashion items, and sweet treats to bring back home as mementos of your Basque adventure.

Afternoon: Depending on your departure time, relax at a cafe enjoying a final cup of "café con leche" (coffee with milk) or explore the banks of the Nervión River for a scenic farewell.

Bonus Tip: Bilbao offers a Bilbao Pass, which provides free entry to many museums, discounts on attractions, and free public transport. Consider purchasing one for the duration of your stay, especially if you plan on visiting several museums and attractions.

CONCLUSION

As you close this book, Bilbao's vibrant energy will likely linger. You've explored the Guggenheim Museum's architectural marvel, wandered the charming Casco Viejo, and tasted the culinary delights of pintxos. But Bilbao is just the beginning.

This Basque city pulsates with a unique rhythm, a captivating blend of tradition and contemporary flair. You've glimpsed its soul through the passionate locals cheering at San Mamés, the rhythmic clatter of txistu flutes filling the air during a festival, and the ever-present aroma of freshly baked bread wafting from hidden bakeries.

Bilbao isn't just a destination; it's a springboard to further adventures. Imagine yourself exploring the dramatic Basque coastline, its rugged cliffs pounded by the Atlantic waves. Picture yourself strolling through enchanting medieval villages nestled amidst rolling green hills. Envision yourself savoring world-class Rioja wines in a vineyard, the sun warming your face.

Bilbao beckons you to lose yourself in its magic. But the Basque Country's rich blend unfolds beyond the city limits. Are you ready to delve deeper?

Book your flight, pack your bags, and prepare to be captivated by the heart and soul of Basque Country. Bilbao awaits.

Printed in Great Britain
by Amazon